SOCIAL LIVES OF
Pigs

Elliot Riley

ANIMAL BEHAVIORS

Rourke
Educational Media

rourkeeducationalmedia.com

Scan for Related Titles and Teacher Resources

Before & After Reading Activities
Level: **J**

Teaching Focus:
Predicting. Text features allow students to access their prior knowledge on the concept by looking at the pictures. Have students practice using the glossary by looking up the bold vocabulary words shown in the text before they read it.

Before Reading:

Building Academic Vocabulary and Background Knowledge
Before reading a book, it is important to set the stage for your child or student by using pre-reading strategies. This will help them develop their vocabulary, increase their reading comprehension, and make connections across the curriculum.
1. Read the title and look at the cover. *Let's make predictions about what this book will be about.*
2. Take a picture walk by talking about the pictures/photographs in the book. Implant the vocabulary as you take the picture walk. Be sure to talk about the text features such as headings, Table of Contents, glossary, bolded words, captions, charts/diagrams, and Index.
3. Have students read the first page of text with you then have students read the remaining text.
4. Strategy Talk – use to assist students while reading.
   - Get your mouth ready
   - Look at the picture
   - Think…does it make sense
   - Think…does it look right
   - Think…does it sound right
   - Chunk it – by looking for a part you know
5. Read it again.
6. After reading the book complete the activities below.

Content Area Vocabulary
Use glossary words in a sentence.

cooperative
dominant
empathy
forage
hierarchy
socializing

After Reading:

Comprehension and Extension Activity
After reading the book, work on the following questions with your child or students in order to check their level of reading comprehension and content mastery.
1. *When pigs connect to the emotions of other pigs, what is it called?* (Summarize)
2. *How do pigs remember and recognize each other?* (Asking questions)
3. *Name some sounds that pigs make. What does each sound mean?* (Text to self connection)
4. *What is a group of wild pigs called?* (Summarize)

Extension Activity
Pig finger painting! With the help of an adult, lay out a piece of finger-painting paper. Place a glob of red and white paint on the sheet. Finger paint a pig with the two colors and discover what color they make when they are mixed together. After your painting dries, cut out your pig shape!

Table of Contents

FAMILY GROUPS

Pigs are smart, social animals. They like to run, relax, and play together.

Wild and domestic pigs begin **socializing** soon after they are born. Newborn piglets establish relationships with their siblings in a **hierarchy.**

Domestic pigs live on farms. They also are sometimes kept as family pets.

This means that the more **dominant** piglets get more milk at feeding time. That pig will often be the biggest in the group. This hierarchy will stay the same as long as the group stays together.

In the wild, pigs live in **cooperative** groups called sounders. Each sounder usually has two to six female pigs, or sows, and their piglets.

The sows protect and nurture their babies. They also care for the other piglets in the group.

Adult male pigs, or boars, typically live alone. Young males leave the family group when they are between seven and 18 months old.

Pig Talk

Pigs communicate through grunts, barks, and squeals. They are known to make more than 20 unique sounds.

A short grunt may mean a pig is excited. A dominant pig may bark a warning at a weaker pig. Pigs also may scream when they are hurt.

In an experiment, one-day-old piglets responded to a recording of their mothers while ignoring the sounds of other pigs.

Pig language also includes jaw chomping, teeth clacking, roars, snarls, and snorts.

FRIENDS FOR LIFE

Pigs are generally friendly animals. They recognize and remember up to 30 other pigs by their scent.

Pigs use odor from urine and the facial glands to identify other pigs.

They greet each other with loud calls and by rubbing snouts.

Pigs in a sounder stay nearby each other most of the time. The hierarchy helps the group maintain harmony. Every pig knows its place.

Pigs show they care for each other in many ways. They like to be in close contact, and will often huddle together to sleep. Pigs also groom each other.

Piglets often form tight bonds with their siblings. These special relationships last into adulthood.

Smart and Sensitive

Scientists have observed many types of pig behaviors. One study showed that pigs connect to the emotions of other pigs. This is called **empathy**.

When one pig is stressed, the others
around it will become stressed.

When one pig is happy, the others will display happy behaviors, such as wagging their tails and barking.

Pigs like to run around, **forage**, and cool off in the mud. But did you know they can also be taught to play video games and pick up their own toys?

A researcher taught domestic pigs to play video games using a special joystick they controlled with their mouths.

These social, emotional animals are among the smartest in the world.

PHOTO GLOSSARY

cooperative (koh-AH-pur-uh-tiv): Animals and people that are cooperative organize activities and roles so that everything functions smoothly.

dominant (DA-muh-nuhnt): Someone or something that is dominant exerts the most power or influence in a group.

empathy (em-PUH-thee): Empathy is the ability to understand and share the feelings of another.

forage (FOR-ij): To forage means to go in search of food. Pigs will often forage for food to feed their young.

hierarchy (HYE-ur-ahr-kee): A hierarchy is an arrangement in a group in which people or animals have different ranks or levels of importance.

socializing (SOH-shul-eye-zing): Socializing means interacting in a group. Pigs learn to socialize with their siblings and other pigs soon after they are born.

INDEX

WEBSITES TO VISIT

http://kids.nationalgeographic.com/animals/pig

www.librarypatch.com/2015/01/10-animal-
research-websites-for-kids.html

www.onekind.org/education/animals_a_z/pig

ABOUT THE AUTHOR

Elliot Riley is an author and animal lover in Tampa, Florida. When she's not writing or watching animal videos, you can find her reading in her favorite hammock or hanging out with her four kids.

Meet The Author!
www.meetREMauthors.com

© 2017 Rourke Educational Media

Library of Congress PCN Data

Social Lives of Pigs / Elliot Riley
(Animal Behaviors)
ISBN 978-1-68191-703-0 (hard cover)
ISBN 978-1-68191-804-4 (soft cover)
ISBN 978-1-68191-901-0 (e-Book)
Library of Congress Control Number: 2016932582

Rourke Educational Media
Printed in the United States of America, North Mankato, Minnesota

PHOTO CREDITS: Cover © Igor Stramyk, cover typography for PIGS © Ron Dale; Pig drawing in stamp art © Yuriy Sosnitskiy; Page 4 © Nut Iamsupasit, Page 5 © Budimir Jevtic, Page 6 © Pakhnyushchy, Page 7 © John Carnemolla; Page 8 © Four Oaks (sow & piglets), Neil Burton (boar), Page 9 © janecat; Page 10 © Sherjaca, Page 11 © UbjsP; Page 12 © Linda George, Page 13 © Jessica Borgenstierna; Page 14 © jadimages, Page 15 © Chrislofotos; Page 16 © Budimir Jevtic, Page 17 © Ajai Alen; Page 18 © BMJ, Page 19 © Antonio V. Oquias; Page 21 © jadimages; page 23 top © taviphoto. All images from Shutterstock.

Edited by: Keli Sipperley

Cover design, interior design and art direction: Nicola Stratford
www.nicolastratford.com

Also Available as: